*15 Top Ways To Save Money*
*How to save on mortgage loans*
*How to save on insurance*
*How to save on home improvement*
*How to save on credit cards*
*Table of Contents*
*How to save on auto loans*
*How to save on phone service*
*How to save on major appliances*
*How to save on home heating and energy*
*How to save on gasoline*
*How to save on car repairs*
*How to save on furniture*

*How to save on clothing*
*How to save on vacations*
*How to save on groceries*
*How to save on prescription drugs*

*How to save on insurance*
*Your life insurance:*
*hundred dollars if you buy insurance from a low-price but licensed*
*opportunity for you to save on insurance. Here are some tips you can*
*-If you prefer just insurance protection, and not a savings and insurer. Compare prices of the insurance departments in your state*
*How to save on insurance*
*interest if there are too many people involved. So negotiate with just*
*-Negotiate a lower selling price with a broker who works for you and not asthe mediator to the seller. There may be a conflict of As much as possible, if it can be done, you must seize every Your home insurance:*
*follow.*
*the broker.*
*and get the lowest price but most practical company.*
*-If you think about it, you can actually save up to several investment life policy, you can just buy term life insurance.*

*-If you would like to purchase whole life insurance, then hold on*

*least not what most people deem it to be. Refinancing means reducing monthly*

*Auto loans gives the buyer the opportunity to refinance their loan at terms that allows them to save their money. However, refinancing is not saving. At*

*to one up to 15 years. If you cancel these policies after only two years*

*history. This is favorable for a buyer who has no negative records on his account*

*whatsoever.*

*A smart investor knows he must seize every opportunity that comes*

*refinancing is appealing to those whose credit scores are of good*

*of having them in your name it will mean double the insurance costs.*

*get one that suits your personal savings.*

*How to save on auto loans*

*-Check the public library about life insurance in your state and*

*How to Save on Auto Loans*

*knocking at his door -asong as it allows him to save more. Auto payments in order to save a litte extra money. Car refinance loans are useful in downsizing.*

*changes as long as there is the approval from the lender and the person applying for*

*must submit an application before any negotiation takes place. Provide the same*

*Auto loans are just a click away, thanks to the Internet. Lenders little off in paying at due time, you will not be able to get the auto specializing in refinancing are online to assist possible clients about auto loans. One*

*options for auto loans are negotiated with the lender beforehand. There can be*

*have a clear record, but that does not mean that because you were a good as opposed to you having a clear record.*

*documents required when making a loan at any bank or establishment.*

*But there are auto loan refinances that do not care even if you have a negative credit history. Refinancing at best rates are available if you Throughout the duration of the loan, there are opportunities to refinance the car loan. If you are opting for refinancing, know that the*

*loan that you are applying for. You still would but the rate won't be as the loan.*

*If you need refinancing as soon as possible, consult with the lender*

*will be able to save more. Auto loan refinancing opens more doors to*

*and where you will be able to save more. You have a right to do so because it is your*

*out there, then you are more aware of which one you should choose -depending on*

*saving because it reduces your monthly payments at the interest rate of your choice.*

*you if the terms you are asking for are favorable for them. The catch*

*the one that works for you best.*

*Here is a tip before you invest in auto loans, what are your goals for*

*and try to work around auto loan refinancing requirements. By updating yourself*

*Refinance car oan specialists are more than willing to cooperate with*

*refinancing? You have to compare with the other auto refinancing*

*is that when you choose to refinance then the rates are lower and you*

*with the services andprograms offered by the various car refinance loan specialists*

*businesses before you fully decide on one. Choose one where you get the best deal*

*money and your investment.*

*For car owners, investing on auto loans is a wise decision because it completely decide on which car to purchase. By arranging the terms and finances*

*involved in the car financing program you are committing to.*
*auto loan refinancing can give him the best deal, making him save the most amount.*
*The former is more secured than the latter. You can consult a tax refinancing agreement, you have to take into consideration all the terms that are*
*Also, by tapping the equity inyour home oan, you wil be able to any other deals, it may sound tempting but that is not usually the case. You may*
*If you want you can approach an independent lender before you gives them better deals. However, before you commit yourself to any You must also be very wary of the zerointerest loans. Just like with be buying a car for $18,000 and pay zero interest for two years through the dealer*
*advisorfor a second opinion.*
*before buying the car, dealer financers will be able to assist the consumer in which*
*and getting a rebate of $3000, but how sure are you that there is no catch on that*
*lower the interest payment when buying a car. That is because the home equity loan*
*can actualy provide a lower rate as opposed to a car loan.*
*offer? If you do take the rebate and finance at the given percent, then who knows*

*you may even save more.*
*How to save on mortgage loans*
*Think twice before you make any decision. Especially since it involves*
*Save on mortgage loans*
*that you signed up for. This is based on the interest rate and the*
*length of mortgage. The shorter the duration of the payment, then the*
*more expensive the bill is on a monthly basis; however, the higher the*
*mortgage loan that is appropriate for your budget.*
*So the best advice anyone can give you is to sign up for the right*
*bill per month, the shorter the time duration of the payment.*
*Mortgage loans are calculated depending on the kind of interest*
*money. Stretch your buck for as long as it would take.*
*It is very important to save especially during these tough times.*
*It's all about the question of how much you can afford.*
*Create a*

*budget and envision, how much can you actually pay in a month.*
*the person isn't yet financially stable, it is better that he rents in the*
*Plus, now that you're a homeowner, you're also required to set aside a*
*your monthly income and the total debt ratio —meaning what you are*
*significant amount of your salary for taxes. Owning a home also means*
*mean time. However, calculations show that the expenditures on rent*
*The housing payment is your total mortgage payment set alongside*
*obligated to pay in the big picture.*
*Think long term. Will you still be earning that particular amount in two,*
*unforeseen accident occurs? How long can you keep on paying the*
*are somehow close to signing up for a home mortgage.*
*But with that comes the responsibility of paying your bills on time.*
*three years time? Do you have enough savingsjust in case an mortgage?*
*This is how some lenders calculate how much they can lend you.*
*That's why there's also the question of —Should I buy or rent?‖ If*
*Also, there's a great sense of pride in owning your own home.*
*paying for utilities such as gas, electricity, water and food.*

*For you to decide, think whether choosing a home is what's*
*loan you're signing up for. Mortgage rates depend on the Wall*
*Street*
*clients. That is how they should advertise a rate. This is done so*
*that*
*checking the interest rate and rate movements of a specific*
*mortgage*
*people who signed up under them will be aware of where their*
*rates*
*suitable for you at this time. Determine if you have enough to*
*actually*
*securities. Keep an eye on the stock market and the mortgage*
*market*
*prevents lenders from hiding fees and for clients to have an open*
*can be seen extensively when the yearly rate is presented. This*
*As much as possible, try to personally meet with the lender.*
*trends to know the secrets on the direction of where your*
*mortgage is*
*afford to buy your own home. If not, then it's better that you rent.*
*Now here's where the mortgage rates come in. Begin by*
*going.*
*relationship with their mortgage dealers.*
*law,mortgage companies are required to disclose the APR to*
*their*
*You must also study the APR or the Annual Percentage Rate. By*
*are going. It represents the real cost of the loan to the borrower*
*and*
*When money is involved, personal arrangements are better*
*because*

*not only can you clarify better, you could also have an idea of what*

*insurance matters in the future.*

*means that you are ready to commit with a lender and the lender is*

*not late. This is to ensure that you won't have a hard time dealing with*

*specific amount from your salary for your mortgage; and, if you can*

*and ask if you can pay for a higher amount.*

*the stock market, and then you are ready to lock in your rate. This*

*kind the person is on the end of the phone or at the receiving part of*

*bound to a promise to this certain interest rate.*

*have any problem with money. It's just having the discipline of the email you send out.*

*pay faster, then why not? If you have extra money, talk to your lender*

*From there, you must work on a budget. You must set aside a*

*For good credit history, always pay more, not less. Pay on time,*

*With the right decision-making and the right budget, you won't*

*Now that you have met up with a dealer, know your APR, study*

*creating a budget, sticking to it and paying on time.*

*If it is arranged as such, notice that you could even save a couple of your dollars.*

*The credit cards make payments and expenses so convenient*

*How to Save on Credit Cards: The Cost-Effective Ways to Bigger*

*Consumers know it more as credit cards. In fact, nearly 81% of*

*plastic as the most convenient tool for shopping and paying utility bills.*

*Statistical reports prove that Americans are in love with plastic.*

*$8,000. That is, indeed, a great amount of debt.*

*that the average credit card balance Americans have amounts to*

*Savings When Times are Tight*

*So if you want to avoid debts and save more on your credit card*

*How to save on credit cards*

*American households have at least one credit card. They find these*

*bills, try to cut back on your expenses and follow the rules on how to save on credit cards.*

*can't afford to pay.*

*Here's how:*

*2. Go for the lowest interest rate*

*that can offer you with reasonable credit limits. In this way, you will*

*the rewards, services, and interest rates that will suit your needs.*

*go the extra mile in shopping expenses, it is best to get a credit card*

*not be tempted to max out your card and accumulate debts you simply*

*Not all credit cards are created equal. There is a particular credit*

*card that will suit your needs. Getting this type of card will provide you*

*If you think you can't pay your credit card bills on time but are willing to pay your balances in another period, it is best to get a credit*

*For instance, if you want convenient shopping but can't afford to*

*1. Choose the best credit card*

*card with lower interest rates.*

*Consumers may not be aware of this, but one of the reasons*

*responsibilities. One of which is to keep a record of all your expenses.*

*Don't get a credit card just because it can provide you with*

*why debts are getting higher is based on the interest rates. The actual*

*several rewards. Not all rewards are worth your time and money.*

*flyer's reward credit card can give you discounts as well as points that*

*prices of airline tickets nowadays.*

*However, it doesn't necessarily mean that you neglect your*

*For instance, a frequent flyer's rewards credit card may not be*

*3. Choose the reward credit cards that suits your lifestyle*

*can be converted into tickets. This will be savings considering the*

*balances are made worse through interest rate charges.*

*functional if you aren't a frequent traveler. But if you are, getting a*

*With credit cards, convenience is the name of the game.*

*4. Keep a record of all your expenses*

*In this way, you will be able to identify which purchases weren't necessary at all. So the next time around, you will know what to avoid.*

*Never let your balances stay on your credit card bill statements*

*card. Financial experts say that cash advances reap higher interest*

*fact, this might trigger further debts. Besides, interest rates only apply*

*rates compared to the ones that you have on your credit card*

*6. Be wary of cash advances*

*try to pay them immediately.*

*Paying your minimum balance only won't do you any good. In*

*5. Do not keep balances*

*expenses for you. If you pay your balances monthly, you won't be*

*purchases, which are, by nature,soaring as well.*

*charged with interest rates, so you get more savings.*

*If it isn't an emergency, never take cash advances on your credit*

*whenever you have balances. And interest rates are additional*

*for long. This means that if you have accrued balances for the month,*

*Combination of these two will definitely bring you to debt* problems. Besides, cash advances don't take on certain periods, so

7. Ask for a lower rate

by requesting their bank or their credit card companies to act

All of these things are catered to help you cut back your

If you have been an obedient customer and pay your bill on

hard if you aren't prepared to pay off your balance immediately.

expenses and save more on your credit cards. These things have been

balances on time.

that means the charges will take place instantly. That would be very

if you are the type of credit card holder who doesn't get to pay the

survey were reported to have trimmed down their interest rates simply

With lower interest rates, you can definitely save more especially

and ask for a lower rate.

accordingly.

time, it wouldn't hurt you to call your bank or your credit card issuer

Surveys show that nearly 55% of those who participated in the

proven effective. It is now up to you if you will heed this advice or not.

*Just remember, your actions will always tell you the kind of life*

*you want to live, so better make good choices and start saving now.*

*groceries. That is simply not saving.*

*your gasoline consumption, you should trim down the refills. There are*

*Saving on gas would mean maximizing the amount of gasoline*

*Managing Oil Prices: Tips on How to Save on Gasoline*

*your car less often in the same way as not eating food just to save on*

*show that your money shouldn't revolve on your gasoline bills alone.*

*If you have been spending more than what you can afford on*

*many things that are more important than just gasoline, so it goes to*

*How to save on gasoline*

*Saving on gasoline won't necessarily mean commuting and using*

*you use, thus, giving youbetter gasoline mileage.*

*Moreover, with the pries of gasoline nowadays, saving more and*

*and without using gasoline, you just have to learn how to maximize*

*If everything is working quite perfectly, you can be sure that you*

*what you have paid for. If you think you can't do away without driving*

*Here are a few reminders:*

*1. A regular tune up on your car can do wonders*

*get better gas mileage, which means less gasoline refills.*

*your gasoline consumption and save more.*

*the vehicle but can also guarantee better gas mileage.*

*gas mileage. The performance will entirely depend on how you*

*You don't have to drive the newest model just to ensure better*

*maintain your car's condition.*

*maximizing your consumption would definitely give you more than*

*A regularly tuned up car will not only mean longer life span of*

*2. Are you a racer?*

*If not, then try to drive a little slower. Driving faster than the wind won't only get you into trouble but can also waste a lot of*

*Experts say that ―traveling velocity‖ can put a great impact on*

*more force and energy and, of course, better gasoline consumption.*

*If your car has a dirty or congested air filter, replacing them will*

*your gasoline use. For example, if you drive at 105kph instead of*

*88kph, you are increasing your gasoline consumption up to 17%. That*

*that is simply overspending.*

*absolutely perk up your car's gasoline mileage up to 10% more.*

*Besides, having clean airfilters all the time will ensure your car*

*3. Be wary of your filter's condition*

*is a lot of gasoline you have there, and when converted into dollars,*

*Filters make your car's engine more cost-effective. It can create*

*gasoline without you knowing it.*

*Filters may seem one of the most neglected parts on a car. Most*

*motorists don't understand the importance of air filters.*

*engine's optimum performance and durability.*

**4. Break it more gently**
Breaking and accelerating more frequently will not only wear out
so that you can apply measured, steady brake.
gasoline you use, and not just because they deteriorate faster.
If your tires are deflating more whenever you drive, you are
manufacturer's instructions. Keep in mind that a tire that has been
consumptionmore than 18%.
than what is recommended. Try to anticipate, as well, the traffic ahead
So whenever you are on the road, try not to accelerate more
It is best to always keep your tires well inflated according to the
your car's condition and tires but can also increase you gasoline
actually taking more money from your pockets.
Why? Simply because the less efficient your tires are, the more
**5. Check your tires**
inflated by 2 PSI can actually boost your car's gas use by 1%.

6. Organize your shopping trips

7. Reduce wind resistance

If you will be driving on a highway, it is best to keep your

you can cut back on fuel use.

can also save more on your expenses.

on gas. Just try to be conscious of where your money goes and it will

All of these things can, in some way or another, help you save

force just to push your car through the wind and this would mean

windows closed so as to lessen that drag. Dragging can aggravate fuel

consumption. Remember your physics? It will definitely take more

and have all your groceries bought on a single day. It would be best if

using more gas than usual.

Consider this: try to budget your food consumption for the week

Getting things organized not only makes life easier to bear but

you can find all of the things you need in a single store. In this way,

be easier for you to find cost-effective ways to save more money.

*How to save on car repairs*

*getting their cars repaired and drain their finances as well? If you are,*

*can afford.*

*without getting it repaired.*

*choosing the right repairs, you can be spending more than what you*

*Guide Book to Savings*

*then it is high time you start looking for ways to save on car repairs*

*You are left with no choice at all but to get it fixed. The only*

*and save more in your piggy bank.*

*Defective cars aren't even worthy to be sold without getting all*

*problem is that without the appropriate guidelines you need in*

*Tips on How to Save on Car Repairs: The Car Owner's Ultimate*

*Are you one of those few people who are having trouble in the necessary repairs. You can't even exchange it with another car*

*With the high prices going on in the market today, no one can* really afford to have their cars repaired in very expensive packages.

save on car repairs:

1. Do your homework

Through research, you can identify the right mechanic and the

your mechanic right way the things that need to be repaired. This will

best mechanic or repair service for their cars.

2. Take note of the things that need to be repaired

prevent unnecessary repairs or misunderstandings on the type of

So you have to think of waysto save more on car repairs.

necessary repairs listed on a piece of paper. In this way, you can tell

ordinary basis without opting to excessive ways. Here's how you can

they spend more on car repairs simply because they didn't choose the

You can trim down on car repairs and save more cash on an

One of the greatest problems most motorists encounter is that

Before you go to your mechanic, it is best to have all the right shop.

repairs that your car needs. Unnecessary repairs will only add up to *your repair expenses.*

*compare prices. In this way, you can evaluate and compare prices*

*job, it is best to have the estimate written on a piece of paper. Try to*

*3. Shop and compare*

*enabling you to find the best quotes possible.*

*accumulation of extra charges, which weren't included on the first*

*This means that before you commit yourself in a particular repair*

*estimation.*

*acquire a copy of your own. This will prevent unnecessary*

*Never grab the first repair shop you find. By looking around, you*

*4. Try to make every transaction in black and white*

*can still find better shops than what you have right now.*

*Keep in mind that not all job repairs were created equal and not*

*To get the best quotes on car repairs, try to shop around and*

*all mechanics are honest. So it is best to protect yourself as always.*

*5. Acquire your car's old parts before you let the mechanic start*

*the next repair.*

*your mechanic take the chance of acquiring these things. You can have*

*this way, you can decide which things need greater considerations.*

*them repaired on some machine shops and cut back your expenses on*

*If you don't know your way around car repairs, it is best to ask*

*There are certain car parts that can still be rebuilt. So never let*

*maintenance. In this way, you will learn some important matters*

*Besides, if you will just let your mechanic decide on your car's*

*regarding car parts. This will enable you to differentiate the important*

*repair process, you might pay more than what you can imagine.*

*someone (definitely not your mechanic) for some second opinions. In*

*Better yet, read some easy-to-read manuals on car the repair process*

*6. Know your way around*

*repairs from those that you can do by yourself.*

*7. Ask for the warranty*
*Some repair shops offer warranties on the services that they*
*you can be sure that your car and your pocket are in good hands.*
*Indeed, car repairs can't be avoided. These are the things that*
*Furthermore, warranties can guarantee high quality repairs so*
*make. Take note of this so that you can be sure not to spend another*
*tune-ups, changing windshield wipers and other simple tasks.*
*hundred dollars for the same repair in just a few days.*
*of knowledge you can handle minor maintenance like oil changes,*
*you have to learn to live with.*
*Finding good repair shops aren't that hard. Just try to remember*
*these pointers and you will surely spend less with car repairs.*
*That's where those manuals may come in handy. With just a little bit*
*Also, think about learning how to do the simple chores yourself.*
*Learning to do these yourself will result in great savings!*

*How to save on home improvement*
*pertains to the method of refurbishing or repairing a home.*
*their home improvements through their own initiative.*
*Home improvement can add sparkle to a dull wall color, a new*
*pretty popular. Through this process, homeowners can enjoy*
*make some improvements in your home and create a*
*difference.*
*Cool Tips on How to Save on Home Improvement*
*No wonder why the so-called ─do-it-yourself‖ jobs have been*
*renovating their own homes like professionals. There are*
*shops that*
*provide seminars or workshops regarding their products and*
*the way*
*shade to a dreary interior design, or vigor to a lifeless porch. It*
*simply*
*fees of ─professional handyman,‖ many people have opted to*
*work on*
*In most cases, an expert executes home improvements.*
*Have you ever thought of changing your room's design? Do you*
*think your porch needs a little makeover? Then it is time for*
*you to*
*However, with the cost of commodities nowadays, plus the real*
*service*
*homeowners can operate them at home.*

There are many types of home improvements. Each category
1. Do your research
type of home improvements.
can provide optimum modernization to one's home.
2. Scout for the best quotes
best to identify the right measures to save more on home
improvement packages available on the market today. It is also best
improvements.
improvement costs:
However, home improvement package prices may vary. It is
do some extensive research. Try to find out the current prices of home
Before you start on your home improvement project, it is best to
Here are some ways on how to cut back on your home
to identify the different factors that can affect the conditions of each
If you will be hiring a professional, it is best to look for the best

price quotes on home improvements. In this way, you will be able to

3. Do the math

improvement, it is best to have everything estimated.

more than what you can afford.

Besides, having a rough estimate of your home improvement

on it, you can now consider the other areas without having to spend

Should you decide to seek the services of a professional you will anticipate the possible rates and charges, which will enable you to

expenses.

Before you start buying things that you need for your home

know how much it will take you to improve your home. You can't tradesman.

prepare the required amount. Get quotes from more than one

plans will enable you to control your expenses. You can focus on the

easily be fooled by anyone because you know exactly the cost of areas that need to be prioritized. Once you have set a specific budget

4. Decide whether you can do it yourself or you should hire a

*professional*

*strategy in marketing. It is also one of the best ways to ask for some*

*help about the things that you are not familiar with.*

*5.Ask for recommendations*

*If you want to save more on your home improvements, it is best start the job.*

*on your home improvement.*

*your expenses, where in fact, you don't have the slightest idea how to*

*destruction. It is best to hire a professional if you really want to save*

*to decide if you can do the project yourself or you really need to hire a*

*Insisting to do the job yourself will only end up in waste or*

*Word of mouth is considered as one of the best advertising*

*For example, if you don't have any idea abouthome*

*professional.*

*It is unwise to assume that you can do the job just to trim down*

*improvements, it is best to ask your friends, relatives, or even*

colleagues about home improvements.
6. Find the best contractor
home improvements can really help you make a difference.
it is best to hire the best. You can do this by checking on your
They can give you some pointers about home improvements
improvement projects. Keep in mind that home improvements need
that the services you pay are reliable and efficient.
based on their own experience. Tried and tested, their idea about
If you wish to save on home improvements through contractors,
Try to keep these things in mind to save on your home
contractor's capabilities and certifications. In this way, you can be sure
not be expensive. You can beautify your home without having to go
How to save on home heating and energy
overboard.
How to Save on Home Heating Energy: Superb Saving Ideas

To say that you can save on your home's heating system and
Everybody longs to reduce his or her expenses on energy and
The greatest reason for this dilemma is the on-going increase of
have control of, such as energy consumption.
phenomenon are things you don't see everyday but desire to
obtain.
electricity bill. In fact, statistical reports prove that heaters are
one of
energy isn't an understatement. Reduced bills on your
electricity,
energy consumption charges. Everything seems to have high
prices
One of the best examples of energy use are home heating
heating systems so as to save on energy consumption as well.
As you
heating systems. People don't work just to pay the utility bills
alone.
For this reason, it is imperative to think of ways to save on
nowadays. It is best to trim down the other expenses in which
you
systems. However, heaters can eat up bigger portions in your
the consumption rate in a given year.
maximized heating system, and a whole lot of energy saving
the largest energy consumers in every home, that is, more than
half of
save on these items, you get more value for your money.

*But how? Things are, most of the time, easier said than done. So*

*will consume less energy.*

*With the solar energy utilized in your home's heating system, you can start heating your water for showers or revolutionize your*

*2. Inspect your home*

*Natural is always the best. To save more on energy, it is best to*

*To help you, here is a list of some energy saving tips that will help you cut back on your furnaces' energy consumption.*

*if you think that it is easy to maximize your heaters and save more on*

*energy, think again.*

*home's heating system and still reduce your electricity bill.*

*system. In this way, you trap natural heat coming from the sun. You*

*use solar energy when using water heaters in your home's heating*

*1. Use solar energy*

*To maximize your home's heating system, it is best to inspect your house for any leakage. Leaks will let the heat seep out from your*

*your furnace by as much as 50%.*

*3. Use heaters on frequently used rooms only*

*To save more energy, only use heaters on areas that are*

*home, thus, absorbing cold from the outside. Most of the areas that*

*4. Insulate*

*possible so as to cut back any unnecessary costs on energy.*

*frequently visited and used by your household. For rooms that are not*

*leakage starts to develop are in the windows, doors, and fireplaces.*

*utilize natural heat.*

*Once identified, it is best to take some proper actions as soon as*

*By doing so, you can cut back your energy consumption through*

*Close the vents to the rooms that you are not using.*

*being used, try to turn off the thermostat or close the windows to*

*One of the biggest secrets in maximizing your home's heating* system is insulation. A properly and well insulated home can guarantee

repair shops and that would be additional expenses for you.

5. Get a good heating system

All of these things can help you maximize your heating system

and other areas that need padding. This will block the heat in and keep

It is best to use some insulating devices on your roof, windows,

Besides, defective products would require frequent visits to

Of course, you can never guarantee lower energy bill if not for

an efficient heating system. A defective heating system can use twice

save more money by cutting back your energy consumption.

use more force just to boost more heat, and the more force the

a comfortable home without using too much energy. Thus, you can

it from escaping the house.

heating device use, the more energy it will consume.

as much energy as one that is functioning properly. The tendency is to

and save more energy. In this way, you can save more money and use

it on other things that need prioritization.

Depending on where you live, consider switching from electric to phone services such as long distance calls.
the telecommunications industry in the United States. In fact, reports
Since its inception, long distance calls have created a niche in more than 1.75% of consumers' general expenses are attributed to
you live in and determine which better meets your needs.
No wonder why many Americans are squanderers when it comes gas or vice versa. Electricity is less costly in some areas while in from the Federal Communications Commission have attested that other areas gas is the better choice. Do your research for the area
to phone services. In 1992, reports show that the average amount
billion.
How to save on phone service
that the Americans spend on long distance calls amount to $10.3
How to Save on Phone Service
Now, the question lies on whether these expenses are

*maintained and paid by the phone companies' subscribers. Come to*

*long distance calls. Each feature is designed to suit the needs of every*

*customer or subscriber.*

*think of it, the utilization of phone services has increased to a level*

*popularity that the phone companies used to have.*

*What happens next is that some phone companies were required*

*phone companies have come up with revolutionary added features that*

*people to subscribe to phone services once more and gain back the*

*But to some, cutbacks aren't the ultimate solution. Most of the*

*where consumers can no longer pay their dues.*

*to make some cutbacks on their operating expenses.*

*VoIP, wireless, and calling cards. Each service has its own pros and*

*are more functional and multidimensional. These items seek to entice*

*The usual phone service options are the bundled, traditional,*

*With these phone companies have created different choices for*

*cons, but all of them were catered to provide optimum phone services*

*to their subscribers.*

*Sounds good enough? Think again.*

*To save more on your phone services, it is best to choose a good*

*With the high prices of commodities nowadays, it pays a lot to provide.*

*But how?*

*available on the market today. Compare their rates and choose the*

*save on your phone services and earn that extra money you will need*

*Here are some few good tips:*

*consumers can find ways on how to save on phone services,*

*equal. And even if they may vary according to their rates and charges,*

*1. Select a good plan*

*in the near future.*

*plan first. You can do this by checking on the phone companies*

*regardless of their classification and the type of service that they*

*First, keep in mind that not all phone services were created*

*best plan.*

However, experts say that it would be better if you choose from

the three leading phone companies in the industry. Statistical reports

Once you have identified them, you can easily detect which

Analyze the flow of calls and pinpoint those that create particular

easier for you to save more on your bills.

patterns.

areas you call frequently, at what time, and for how long.

show that you can save by as much as 50% or more as compared to

So if you have clearly identified your calling pattern,‖ it will be

3. Flexibility

2. Identify your ‒calling pattern‖

other phone companies.

Try to identify your calling pattern based on the latest three bills.

Choose a phone service that gives you the flexibility to adapt to

your needs. This will guarantee optimum communication service

because you can alter or modify any feature that will correspond to
only to find out that you get double charges in return after the
some promotions that may only lure to try a particular phone service,
promotion is over.
4. Be wary on the promotions
post-paid long distance phone service and you wish to convert your
phone service into prepaid, it is best to choose a long distance carrier
In this way, you can save on the service fees (for the
With this, you not only passed the chance of saving more money
your needs.
can now control your long distance activities.
For example, if you have been previously subscribed to a
Not all freebies and promotions can be good for you. There are
that will allow you to do such thing without the extra charges.
conversion) as well as on the long distance charges. With prepaid, you
on your phone services, but you also missed the chance to enjoy real
savings without having to spend more than what you can afford.

*Indeed, saving on phone services can trim down your expenses*

*Saving is one of the most important things to consider in appliances such as fridge, washing machine, stove, and heater.*

*How to save on major appliances*

*an independent planning to move to a different place, saving should*

*For example, moving into a new area requires basic household*

*appliances.*

*would not consider some of the cost-effective tips in buying major*

*in a month. It is best to remember these pointers very well as they*

*budgeting. Whether you are a parent of two or three or a student or*

*may come in handy sometime in the future.*

*Normally, these appliances would cost you thousands of dollars if one*

*Your Guide to Saving on Major Appliances*

*always be put as a number one priority.*

*With that being said, below are just some of the cost-effective* and saving tips in purchasing new appliances for your new abode.

part of our daily lives but with a starter, one would have to evaluate

of thinking in order to keep all those that are important and set aside

a.Evaluate your Wants and Needs. Appliances will always be

While these add-ons are important, this should also require a lot

wise to purchase a huge refrigerator when you only have few square

those that will provide luxury. Worth mentioning is the amount of

and think about the most important household appliances to buy.

For families, parents should also take into consideration the type

sofa or a convenient ice-making machine against a reasonable fridge?

to a new house. Would you prefer buying a fridge in favor of a new

inches of space available for your immediate kitchen needs.

electricity that one has to consume when using these add-on products.

appliances can be fun if you have enough or available space. It isn't

First, think about the things that you should need when moving

b.Size –accommodating your newly purchased electrical

of appliances, which will be able to supply all the needs for the family.

*A 5.0-kilogram washer would definitely not suffice in a family of 5. In*

*better than procuring a new one specially when one would look into*

*accommodate most of the clothing used for a week by a single person*

*Basically, for people who are determined to make the purchase, comparing prices on the market before doing the actual buying and*

*More often than not, leveraging on secondhand appliances is*

*c.Consult with Comparison Shops. The 1999 Consumer*

*such cases, one would have to consider purchasing those that are of*

*compare price around before they do the actual purchasing on major*

*alone.*

*they would usually shop on a single appliance center and don't bother*

*to shop around and compare prices at nearby stores.*

*Literacy Consortium report provides enough reason for consumers to*

*The consumer report provided information about the benefits of heavy-duty type of major appliances.*

*You will save more on buying in bulk than for one that won't appliances.*

*the importance of shopping online for auctions and sales.*

*similar features and durability standard. This intelligent buying will* save you hundreds of dollars as expected and allot savings toother

appliances. It's about how you would search the local market and the

records of buying guides and ratings and prices on some of the major

prices from coast to coast and details on handling and packaging of

your family.
features and performance match specifically to the needs and wants of

appliances nationwide. These buying guides and consumer literacy

net to find shopping exclusives and sales of appliance items whose

d. Annual Buying Guide −Local libraries today keep some
The report also maintains a database where you can compare
(durability), price, and quality among other things.
e. Where to Buy −Sometimes, it isn't about the name of the
home stuffs that in turn provides additional luxury in your part.
reports provide exclusive and substantial information on performance
merchandises should one would interest on buying them.
merchandiser that matters when filling your home with major
These buying techniques won't only free you on your budget but

provide you additional leverage on saving for future appliance needs.

lies in your ability to making compromises.

How to save on furniture

Tips On How To Save On Purchasing Your Furniture

doesn't necessarily mean sacrificing the quality of the product. Of

customer asks for it and when one is purchasing refurbished items.

course, you want only the best worth for your very own home. The

f.Negotiate –In almost every part of the selling process,

item after making a careful review of its features. Getting the best bet

1. Look for Furniture on SALE!

Saving money on purchasing your furniture for your home

money when you procure your dream furniture:

Most stores would drop prices when needed and when the negotiation takes place when you would interest on purchasing the

following are keys and tips that you can follow to save an awful lot of

More often than not, the best deal on Furniture on Sale comes every January and July. And if you're looking for outdoor furniture,

people and pay them by commission.

advantage of their eagerness.

these lines of products will be offered at a very low price. Another

These people will definitely have their own bills to pay so would

be a little more desperate to make the sale, hence, could be giving a

sole purpose of their clearance.

better deal for your most wanted furniture. You can definitely take

have their furniture set on very low prices every end of the month for

This means that at the end of the month, there will be certain introducing new furniture.

August is the best time ever! Also, mostof the furniture companies

basis, computing their sales, releasing their promotions and

Majority of the retail furniture companies function on monthly

pieces of furniture that won't be offered the following month, thus

reason will be because most of the furniture companies hire sales

2. Visit your Favorite Furniture Stores

*Check all the possible Furniture Shops first and find the best deal*

*deal!*

*using the money that you have allotted for the furniture; this will save*

*Then, you may pay for your credit card bill the following day returned merchandise is being sold at low prices.*

*this credit card and you can get discounts for your desired piece of*

*These credit cards normally give you the best discounts on the furniture inside that furniture center. All you have to do is apply for*

*know when the right furniture is going to be waiting for you at its best*

*before finally purchasing your piece. Most regional and national*

*3. Apply for the Credit Card being offered by the Furniture Shop*

*fixture.*

*furniture retailers haveoutlet shops where suspended, distressed and*

*Form a habit of checking these shops frequently —you never Some wholesale furniture shops offer in-store credit cards. you the finance charge that the credit card company may cost you.*

4. Search the World Wide Web
After seeing a certain piece of furniture either at the store near
well. Use the famous search engines like Google and Yahoo.
If you live within a few miles of a furniture manufacturer, it is
furniture at a very good discount. However, it is imperative to check
you or in a certain magazine, check the Net for this certain product.
lowest possible price for your preferred furniture.
strongly suggested that you visit their shops for you may get the
the shipping rates and taxes that may be applied with the product.
may mislead you on possible additional charges.
Please don't just rely on the price that is posted on the initial site for it
There are some Online Shops that may offer your certain
Just enter the manufacturer's name and if that piece has its name as
5. Go Directly To The Manufacturer
6. Buy Used Furniture

*One of the best ways of saving your hard-earned money is by*
*carpenter to put the touch of your individuality and giving it the*
*smell*
*More often than not, the total price of your furniture plus the*
*trends come and go as the seasons. It is very possible to save*
*money*
*cities.*
*How to save on clothing*
*tactics on how you can save your money. Here are some tips on*
*how*
*Saving Guide on Clothing*
*Stores selling used furniture are almost everywhere especially in*
*major*
*Clothes can be really costly, especially when all the fads and*
*when buying your clothes. You just need to have the strategies*
*and*
*cost of the repair is still a lot cheaper than buying a totally new*
*piece.*
*of novelty.*
*going to Second Hand shops for certain furniture. You may opt to*
*have your fixture reupholstered or refinished by your favorite*
*to save when buying your clothes:*

Don't buy in Season clothes –different line of clothes come
·Wait for Factory Sales –when Factories put out their sale
getting quality clothes are much higher than those garage sales
that
·Garage Sales –these are very popular stores and places
clothes at very high prices and normally they go down after a
few
months. Key is just patience to wait.
released, however, after a month, normal Sale or bargain prices
will
Imagine how big this saving is! Also, going directly to the
every season. And more often than not, they normally release
new
season, clothes can be cut from 40%-90% off the original price.
garage sales that are put up by families, in this way, chances of
you can still wear these clothes during the remaining days of
winter
Manufacturer's store is a helpful tip on getting a good deal on
clothes.
For example, when winter comes, coats and sweaters are
now be tagged on these clothes. If you were smart enough to
wait,
and the coming fall.
where you can get your clothes at really, really low prices. Find
have been put up for commercial purposes already.

However, it is important to remember and avoid buying clothes
clothes, and the concept of saving is put to waste.
original price of your desired clothes.
·Bargain –always visit your favorite store and befriend the
·Buy two different sizes and two different colors –If you
you can online shop.
and bargain wherein you can save at a minimum of 20% off the
just because the prices are really low, you might not even wear the
have kids, it is very advisable to actually get two sizes, since children
·Shop Online –nowadays, there are many clothing stores
SALE and BARGAINS as well. Just make a habit of checking regularly
Like the regular stores, the online shops have their season for
online. And, most of the clothing lines have their own websites where
clothes are already at their reduced rates.
grow up really fast. Also, buying two colors to have variety, only if the
sales people there. You can then ask for the possible dates of SALE
your favorite clothing line to wait for these awaited bargains.

Sign up for your Favorite Boutique's mailing list —be sure
Google and you will be given a list of sites that could provide you best
and www.keycode.com.
you will be given your choices of retailers. Youcan also put the —online
your own, especially if you have a favorite store where you frequently
store. Some of the coupon code sites are the www.couponcabin.com
coupon‖ or —coupon code‖ in your favorite search engines such as
in-storecredit cards. All you need to do is apply for a credit card of
could give youa cut off of the original price of your favorite online
catalogs. In this way, you will be updated and be the first one to know
·In-Store Credit Cards —many boutiques nowadays, offer
All you have to do is look for the —apparel‖ category code and clothes as well.
·Coupon Codes and Coupon Cards —if shopping online is
of the upcoming On Sale Items and the new releases of the trendy
to sign up for your favorite clothing store's mailing list, newsletter and
your thing, there are many coupon codes that can be found online that
deals for your retailers.
buy your clothes. Normally, these credit cards give good discounts on

clothes being sold in that particular boutique.
·Get a part-time job at your favorite store −a lot of
the clothes being sold in that particular store.
counterbalance the savings you intentionally wanted in applying for
an awful lot of finance fees and interests. It may not even
the credit card.
new arrival of clothes and rebates. However, this tactic only is
get a minimum of 5% up to 15% discounts.
purchased the product. This is because credit card companies charge
shoppers apply and get part time jobs on their favorite boutique. This
Also, the cardholders normally get special coupons, birthday
discounts and other relative discounts every holiday and often you can
Another benefit of these is free shipping, being updated of the
beneficial if you plan to pay your credit card bill a day after you have
will give them extra money for their job and employee's discounts on
How to save on groceries

*Save Money on Your Grocery Shopping*
*grocery stores when they are hungry. This is the reason why some*
*·Make sure you aren't hungry before you go to the Grocery*
*make you hungry. And this could make you shop and spend more than*
*flexible the budget for the groceries could be. This flexibility should*
*Here are tips on how you can save money for your groceries:*
*budget for the groceries could make or break your budget for your*
*grocery shops have their bakery along the entranceof the store.*
*weekly funds that should be allotted on other things. This is how*
*what you intended.*
*empty, if no food can be taken; drink at least a glass or two of water.*
*One of the basic necessities is your stock of groceries. And your*
*The best way to handle this is to make sure your stomach is not*
*The smell of the freshly baked breads and cakes could really*
*Store −studies have shown that shoppers tend to buy more in the*
*be handled properly.*
*Shopping when you're full will help you combat the temptations of the*

mouth-watering smells inside the grocery store.
·Shop alone —try to find time to go to the grocery store by
you feel tired, you tend to buy more sweets, chocolates and
high-carbohydrates. And when you are mad, you tend to buy more
·Shop when you are in a good mood —when you shop and
or generic brands are either located below or higher than your
average
are normally located on the shelves on your chest level. The
cheaper
to the grocery store early in the morning, you tend to finish with
your
you search the higher and lower shelves. The more expensive
brands
list a little faster, thus avoiding the need to roam around and get
junk food.
sight.
·Try to look up and down on the shelves —make sure that
attracted to unnecessary expenses.
·Go to the store at the early time of the day —when you go
yourself. When you ask for helpers, they tend to increase your bill.
Don't buy non-grocery items —grocery stores normally sell some

non-grocery items like contact lens and painkillers. These products
goodies that you buy. Sometimes they lack a little pound or weigh less
your calculator. In this way, you can easily compute how much you
dealers involved, the cheaper, fresher and better quality of food that
save when buying in-packs or individually wrapped items.
Buy foods that are fresh, cheap and seasoned. With fewer
no matter how much you avoid them. Remember that every cent
you can get for your family.
·Check your receipts after shopping, mistakes can happen
Make sure to double-check the weights of the pre-packed
than what they normally should. Make it a point that you get all your
counts.
hard-earned money's worth.
normally cost more at the grocery stores.
When you specifically went to your favorite grocery shop for a
·Always bring your calculator –make sure to shop with
definite item on sale and suddenly knowing that it's no longer

available. Make sure that you make a rain check and ask for the next
the store.
Don't be misled with the brilliant colored packaging of the
·Check the ends and edges of the grocery store. More
happens, you didn't get the bargain no matter how cheap it seemed.
only what you need. Sometimes, you get deceived when you get to
often than not, the healthy and fresher foods are located at the ends
of the grocery shops. Fruits, vegetables, Dairy products and meats are
normally where the products are very expensive and cost more.
buy things that are on sale even if you don't need them. If this
It's important to focus on the price of the item. Make sure to
examples of these.
stocks to arrive. So that you'll be early the next time the stocks reach
grocery shops. They normally pack certain items simply to attract.
Avoid walking thru the main areas, since these regions are
check the other brands to be certain of getting the best deal. Also, buy
Focus on your list and buy things that you need.

*How to save on vacations*
*from other things like clothes, appliances and groceries, you and your*
*However, it is still imperative to save as much as you can while*
*agencies in your area, make sure to scout for the best deal for ticket*
*cheaper than those of the day flights.*
*ahead of time. Airlines normally have promos if you purchase your*
*It is true that after all saving and cutting down all the expenses*
*Here are the ways on how you can save on your vacations:*
*Save on Airfares –Make arrangements and book your flights*
*family deserves a well planned vacation at least once a year.*
*often than not, the budget is a tough thing to keep.*
*tickets in advance. Also, Airline tickets sell evening flights a little*
*Save on your Vacations*
*If you are purchasing your Airline tickets from the travel*
*having your vacation. Especially, while you are on vacation, more*
*prices. When buying tickets for your family or for four or more*

passengers, there will be special discounts, be sure to ask for these
before leaving for vacation.
Don't forget an auto-check up from your favorite and trusted mechanic
peak seasons. Airfares and hotel accommodation are muchcheaper
cheap gasoline stations and avoid unplanned stops along the way.
The travel agency has its peak and off-peak seasons. Make sure to
opportunities to save.
your tour. Car rentals can be really expensive and unnecessary.
during the lean seasons.
research these dates. Every destination has its own determination of
supermarkets. Eating and dining out in restaurants can be really
For road/land trips, as much as possible, bring your own car for
Don't forget to fill your gas tank. This will allow you to shop for
expensive especially if you are traveling in groups.
·If possible, plan your vacation during the off-peak seasons.
Make sure to bring packaged snacks that are purchased at
Don't pay for your vacation in credit unless you are very certain

that you can pay on time. Interests on such credit can be a burden

Prepare proper clothes to bring for the destination. Buying relatives or close friends can help you save on your vacation. You can

vacation. Discontinue your newspaper deliveries. Temporarily cancel

Don't forget to turn off ongoing expenses while you're away on

Always keep your receipts and track your records for all the

also choose paid accommodations with cooking facilities. This can help

spend your vacation money on other important things.

expenses during the vacation. These can help for future vacations

off your gas and electric heater when you are away from home.

emergency clothes for cold climate can be really costly and should be

·Planning in advance can help you save with your budget.

and can also be deductibles for taxes if you are on business trips.

avoided since you can pack all these from home. In this way, you can

your internet service when on vacation for more than a month. Turn

especially after having fun on your vacation.

·Plan for your Accommodation –considering homes of

you save money from eating out at restaurants. Take advantage of

special offers from hotels or motels offering ―family‖ rates.
Don't forget to budget your money for your souvenir
allowance.
hotelsare really expensive.
Be sure to take advantage of free tourist attractions such as
only charge you minimal fee for your stay, and some even let
you rent
·Consider an adventure trip or ―camping‖ vacation. This is
medicines, alcohol, and stuffs that can heal minor bruises and
cuts.
parks, museums, free gardens and monuments.
Be sure to have portable irons when traveling. Press jobs at
the
your tents. The idea of marshmallows with hotdogs on your
bonfire
can be really exiting.
Don't buy unnecessary souvenir items that can only be sold at
your
garage sale the following year. Buy something useful.
Don't forget to bring your first aid kit that should contain,
really cheap and fun. Some national parks and forest
campgrounds
·Leave and entrust your pets to your friends or families

*instead of bringing them along.*
*How to save on prescription drugs*
*Save on your Prescription Drugs*
*and look into other possibilities which will help you accomplish the task*
*more potent yet approved products by the government.*
*to twenty five percent annually between 1996 and 1999.*
*on saving.*
*Americans are using more prescription drugs at a younger age.*
*Oftentimes, people resorted to ineffective medical products in favor of*
*A recent national study on prescription drugs show that most percent of the senior citizens aren't covered by any insurance inclusive*
*There are many money-saving tips in purchasing prescription*
*The same thing applies to seniors. It shows that more than fifty drugs and one way to doing this is to go through all your resources*
*The study revealed that the Americans spending have increased of medicine benefits specifically for prescription drugs.*

*The following tips provides the best recommendations for saving medicines.*

*average cost of each medicine. Most pharmacies don't offer generic*

*saved from the cost of the initially prescribed medicine by your*

*of the drug prescribed to you. Up to fifty percent or more can be*

*discounts especially from mail-order pharmacy discounts. Check the*

*on prescription drugs and how one would be able to manage to keep*

*a)Go for Generics -Don't forget to request the generic brand*

*b)Make Comparisons -Make sure to compare the prices from*

*Some pharmacies can offer certain discounts on specific brands of*

*different pharmacies before finally purchasing. Values can really vary.*

*c)Look for Discounts -Members of AARP can receive*

*Using the generic brand of medicine can help you save on the*

*them fresh and save on future need of such drugs.*

*brands unless specifically asked.*

*doctors.*

*Veterans Administration to check if you are eligible for some veterans'*

*benefits.*

d)Keep Drugs Away from Sunlight. Make sure to store your
control of your own health. And most doctors even expect you to ask
f)Assess yourself -It is imperative to keeping a daily
||record|| of your physical health. It is really easy to research on your
medicines and pills away from moisture and heat to ensure the optimal
for less expensive brands of the medicines written on your
You are the only one responsible for your health; it is necessary
are taking.
e)Talk to your Doctor -It is definitely okay to ask and inquire
prescriptions.
destroyed and thereby losing its original chemical effect on the body.
potency of these drugs. Most drugs, when exposed to sunlight, tendto
This happens because the very chemical nature of the drug is
that you are well informed of all the medicines and medications you
lose their potency.
to your doctors about the medicines prescribed to you. You are still in
medical condition over the Internet. Maximize your resources.

*Comply with the treatment plan that you and your physician*
*a very minimal difference on the price of the 40 mg to the 80 mg.*
*h)Ask for the samples. A lot of pharmaceutical companies*
*dividing the drug cost in half. One way to do this is through literally*
*They are very eager to let people try their products.*
*g)Double it Up -The fastest way to saving money is by*
*For example, if your doctor prescribed you a 40 mg dosage, you*
*You can save by doing this technique.*
*supply their pharmacies with more than enough of sample medicines.*
*existing illness.*
*can buy the 80 mg tablet and just split it in half. This is since there is*
*have designed for your health. Carefully and specifically following this*
*All you have to do is ask your pharmacists. This can be really*
*plan can help you save money and avoid future recurrence of the*
*safe for short-term illnesses, and could help you save money before*
*cutting a drug in half to attain the exact dosage desired.*
*buying.*

i)Know what your medical insurancecovers. Make sure
certain pre-approved drugs.
Be specific of the maximum amount of your co-payments will pay for
of the plan will definitely vary.
the whole year. More often than not, a health plan only approves for
that you fully understand its coverage before signing up with the plan.
signing up for the plan. Open formularies present more drugs but cost
sure to discuss this with your physician, some medicines aren't
Don't forget to consult your family doctor before completely
j)It costs less to buy your medicine in bulk. However, make
advisable to be purchased in bulk.

www.ingramcontent.com/pod-product-compliance
Lightning Source LLC
Chambersburg PA
CBHW080916160726
48000CB00009B/3011